W9-CLE-679

PENGUIN
SPECIALS

Penguin Specials fill a gap. Written by some of today's most exciting and insightful writers, they are short enough to be read in a single sitting – when you're stuck on a train; in your lunch hour; between dinner and bedtime. Specials can provide a thought-provoking opinion, a primer to bring you up to date, or a striking piece of fiction. They are concise, original and affordable.

To browse digital and print Penguin Specials titles, please refer to **www.penguin.com.au/penguinspecials**

The Silver Way

China, Spanish America and
the Birth of Globalisation,
1565–1815

PETER GORDON

JUAN JOSÉ
MORALES

PENGUIN BOOKS

UK | USA | Canada | Ireland | Australia
India | New Zealand | South Africa | China

Penguin Books is part of the Penguin Random House group of companies
whose addresses can be found at global.penguinrandomhouse.com.

Penguin
Random House
PENGUIN BOOKS

First published by Penguin Group (Australia) 2017

3 5 7 9 10 8 6 4

Text copyright © Peter Gordon and Juan José Morales, 2017

The moral right of the authors has been asserted.

All rights reserved. Without limiting the rights under copyright reserved above,
no part of this publication may be reproduced, stored in or introduced into
a retrieval system, or transmitted, in any form or by any means (electronic,
mechanical, photocopying, recording or otherwise), without the prior written
permission of both the copyright owner and the above publisher of this book.

Cover design by Bi Yabin © Penguin Group (Australia)
Text design by Steffan Leyshon-Jones © Penguin Group (Australia)
Printed and bound in Hong Kong by Printing Express

penguin.com.au

ISBN: 9780734399434

FSC
www.fsc.org
MIX
Paper from
responsible sources
FSC™ C012285

GARY PUBLIC LIBRARY

CONTENTS

A Note on Names 1

Prologue 3

I   A Renaissance Space Race 7

II   The First Transoceanic Shipping Line 20

III   The Emergence of the Global Economy 31

IV   The First World City 40

V   A Global Currency 49

VI   The Birth of Globalisation 64

VII   Ruta Redux 75

Conclusion 80

Timeline 85

Notes 87

Bibliography 92

Illustrations 97

Acknowledgements 98

3 5222 03195 0921

GARY PUBLIC LIBRARY

A Note on Names

The kings of Spain and navigators are referred to by the names to which they are most commonly referred to in English, e.g. Charles and Philip rather than Carlos and Felipe, Columbus rather than Colón, Magellan rather than Magallanes or Magalhães. When spellings differ, e.g. Legaspi and Legazpi, we have chosen the one in more common contemporary use.

The term 'Spanish America' is used to refer those parts of the Americas under Spanish rule during the period in question, roughly the sixteenth century through the first one or two decades of the nineteenth century.

The majority of the diverse primary Spanish and Filipino sources are given in translation in the magisterial fifty-five-volume set *The Philippine Islands, 1493–1898*, edited and annotated by Emma Helen

Blair and James Alexander Robertson, published by the A.H. Clark Company starting in 1903. Almost all of these have been digitised and are available online at www.gutenberg.org and elsewhere. These volumes, or rather the translations, have a small number of idiosyncrasies, such as the use of 'España' for Spain and certain ethnic terms that have since fallen out of favour. These have been updated here.

Prologue

Andrés de Urdaneta is a name that few other than specialist historians will immediately recognise. He was one of the last of the fifteenth and sixteenth century explorers and navigators from the Iberian peninsula whose voyages resulted in redrawing the globe in more or less the form we know it today. Christopher Columbus has a country and several cities named after him; Ferdinand Magellan has the famous straits. But Urdaneta has no such monuments.

Perhaps this is because Urdaneta didn't discover how to get anywhere, but rather less glamorously but no less importantly discovered how to get *back*. Until 1565, no ship had succeeded in sailing east from Asia back across the Pacific to the Americas. It was Urdaneta, a survivor of earlier expeditions, who first worked out the right winds and currents across the uncharted waters of this vast ocean. His discovery was called the *tornaviaje*, or 'return trip'.

The importance of this achievement was well understood at the time: the King of Spain had made it an explicit objective of the voyage, and Urdaneta's arrival in Mexico was cause for public celebration. A letter of the time said that 'those of Mexico are mighty proud of their discovery, which gives them to believe that they will be the center of the world.'[1] They were, as we shall see, arguably correct in this belief.

The trading route that resulted from Urdaneta's discovery – that of the Manila galleons – brought the silver from the Americas that underpinned China's money supply and transformed the global economy. This Ruta de la Plata – or 'Silver Way' – characterised a period when commerce between China and Spanish America formed the lynchpin of trade routes spanning four continents. It also marked the first time the entire world had been knitted together with the global trade and financial networks that form the basis of our modern globalised world and ushered in the global economy that remains with us today.

Urdaneta's discovery and its lasting significance seem largely forgotten, at least in the English-speaking world, among the dustier shelves of the historical record. Yet today's tightly-linked, globalised world derives its origins not so much from the Industrial

Revolution as from this earlier period. The pivotal role of Spanish America and China in these previous 250 years of global integration has been obscured and superseded by the prevailing narrative of Anglo-American predominance in everything from the economy to technology to military power.

Yet China is an increasingly square peg in this round narrative hole. China is, however, more easily accommodated by moving the start of the narrative back by two centuries to a period before New York and London were financial capitals – to, indeed, a period before the United States even existed.

I

A Renaissance Space Race

'History is written by the winners.'
– George Orwell, *As I Please*
4 February 1944[1]

For a period of twelve years starting in 1957 with the launch of Sputnik, the United States and the USSR engaged in a competition for prestige and new expanses whose military and commercial potential was as yet mere speculation. The United States 'won' this space race, landing men on the moon in 1969. Sputnik was a wake-up call, but America's dominance in space has meant that John Glenn, Neil Armstrong and Sally Ride are household names, and not just in the United States. Meanwhile, with the possible exception of Yuri Gagarin cosmonauts such as Alexey Leonov are largely recognised only by Russians and specialists.

By the late fifteenth century, Spanish and Portuguese rulers had been jostling each other for years. Just as the United States and the Soviet Union united against

Germany in the Second World War, these two strategic competitors had a common enemy – in their case, the Muslims who had ruled much of the Iberian peninsula since the eighth century. The strategic competition between Spain and Portugal intensified once the Muslim threat receded and Spain was unified under a single crown.

Portugal had by then been inching down the coast of Africa for several decades, something that didn't much matter if Africa, as some suspected, went on forever southwards. Spain's 'Sputnik moment' came in 1488 when the Portuguese explorer Bartolomeu Dias sailed around the Cape of Good Hope at Africa's southern tip, making his the first European ship to enter the Indian Ocean and thereby open a clear route to the silks and spices of the East.

Asian spices – in particular pepper, but also cloves, nutmeg and others – had driven international trade for millennia. Literally worth more than their weight in gold, no cargo packed more value into as little space. Individual peppercorns could be used as currency. The spice routes from Asia to Europe had long been controlled by Muslim powers. They were subject to disruption, while Europeans powers and merchants were also denied the profits that would accrue from direct access to the sources.

Dias's discovery was very much on the minds of Spain's 'Catholic Monarchs' Ferdinand and Isabella when they famously agreed to finance Christopher Columbus's 1492 voyage to reach Asia by sailing west. Columbus, of course, ran into a new continent, while Vasco da Gama made it to India by 1498. Just a decade later, the Portuguese had established themselves in Southeast Asia and made direct contact with China in 1513, the same year the Spanish explorer Vasco Núñez de Balboa first set eyes on the Pacific Ocean and Ponce de León set foot in Florida. The Americas ended up presenting Spain with opportunities beyond measure, but Spain didn't know that yet – the defeat of the Aztecs and the conquest of Mexico still lay a few years in the future. The Portuguese were trading in China while the Spanish had hardly ventured beyond the Caribbean.

When Columbus died in 1506, it must have been less than evident that it would be his name, rather than Dias's or da Gama's, that would adorn a country, an American holiday, many cities and several universities. Both Dias and da Gama at least had some idea where they were going and where they were once they got there; it is unclear whether Columbus ever realised he had not made it to Asia. And it was Portugal, not Spain, that ruled such transcontinental commerce as there was.

But of course, Spain did conquer both the Aztecs and the Incas, establishing viceroyalties based around

Mexico (known as Nueva España or New Spain) and Peru, and acquiring in the process an empire the size and wealth of which the world had never seen.

Columbus was followed by Vasco Núñez de Balboa, the first European to set sight on the Pacific Ocean; the Conquistadors Hernán Cortés and Francisco Pizarro; and then Ferdinand Magellan, who was ironically Portuguese and whose expedition was the first to circumnavigate the globe, even if Magellan himself didn't make it, having been laid low during an altercation in the Philippines.

Few English speakers could name Magellan's successors, García Jofre de Loaísa, who made the second crossing of the Pacific in 1526 or Ruy López de Villalobos, who named the Philippines in the 1540s. The next explorer who comes up in the conventional narrative is the Englishman Sir Francis Drake, who circumnavigated the globe between 1577 and 1580 before defeating the Spanish Armada in 1588. While a hero to the English, the Spaniards considered Drake a pirate. But once Drake enters the narrative, Anglo-American protagonists tend to dominate.

Loaísa's Asian expedition is important to our story not because it was a success – it wasn't, the fleet was scattered and most of the ships and crew, including Loaísa himself, were lost – but because one of the few who survived was Andrés de Urdaneta. Shipwrecked

An early map of Southeast Asia by Matthias Quad (Cologne, 1600)

in 1526 in the Spice Islands where he was forced to remain for the better part of a decade, contending with the Portuguese who were already there, Urdaneta only returned to Europe in 1536 under guard on a Portuguese ship.

With the race still on, Urdaneta was stripped of his charts and documents once he arrived in Lisbon. However, he managed to escape to Spain and recreate most of the material from memory.

In the subsequent decades, Urdaneta settled in Mexico, took religious orders in 1553 and became an Augustinian friar. A few years later, the new Spanish king, Philip II, wanted another shot at the riches of Asia: among other things, the prices of cloves and other spices, in particular

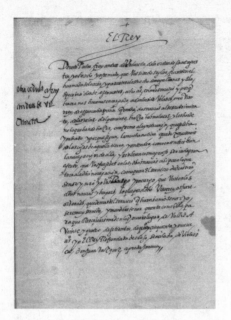

Letter from Philip II to Andrés de Urdaneta. Note 'El Rey' (the King) at top, and the salutation 'Devoto Padre fray andres de Urdaneta'

pepper, were spiralling upwards. And it was to Mexico that Philip wrote Urdaneta personally on 24 September 1559: 'Because of the great knowledge that it is said that you have of the things of that land and your deep understanding of their navigation, and being a good cosmographer, it would be of great help if you would go with these ships not only with regards to the aforementioned navigation but for the service of Our Lord.'[2]

The expedition was to be led by Urdaneta's friend and relative, Miguel López de Legazpi.

*

First page of the Treaty of Tordesillas (1494, Portuguese version)

The similarities between what has become known as the 'age of discovery' and the 'space age' are more than rhetorical. Transoceanic voyages could take years to plan and months if not years to undertake. Missing a departure window could delay a voyage by a year. Should something go wrong, rescue missions were unlikely. Many voyages were, like some proposed Mars missions, one-way. Communications were tenuous.

The planning for Urdaneta's voyage took several years, and the fleet did not depart Puerto de la Navidad on Mexico's west coast until November 1564. The voyage took place under the shadow of what seems today like the most bizarre of legal disputes. Spain and Portugal had been squabbling for years about who had the right to sail and trade where, so in 1494 they decided – after some meddling by the Borgia Pope Alexander VI – to divide the world between them in the Treaty of Tordesillas. A line was drawn 370 leagues west of the Portuguese-controlled Cape Verde Islands. Everything east of the line, at about 46° 37'W, went to Portugal. Everything, that is, except Europe since lands with 'Christian kings' were exempt. This gave Portugal all of Asia and the part of what is now Brazil that sticks out into the Atlantic. Meanwhile, everything west of the line went to Spain, granting them most of what came to be called, a few years later, the Americas. And that was that.

Or at least it was until the Portuguese discovered the Moluccas, part of the Spice Islands. The Spice Islands, so named because they were at the time the sole source of nutmeg, mace and cloves, were also coveted by the Spanish, who knew they could reach them by continuing to sail west to Asia – hence the purpose of the Magellan expedition. Spain argued that the line went all around the globe; Portugal argued that it didn't. But since Emperor Charles V had wars to fight and had as yet no way of getting any spices back to Europe, Spain signed away the islands for 350 000 gold ducats. An anti-meridian was drawn 297.5 leagues east of the Moluccas in the 1529 Treaty of Zaragoza. Urdaneta was, ironically, stranded in the Moluccas when they were sold out from under him.

Both the Spanish and the Portuguese crowns found it convenient and advantageous to follow and enforce the treaties as far as was practicable in their respective areas of influence. The Philippines, as Urdaneta pointed out in a letter to the king, were indisputably on the Portuguese side of the line. Urdaneta departed under the impression that they were heading for New Guinea, as the detailed orders were kept under seal until the expedition was well out to sea. When opened, the destination proved to be the Philippines – Philip, presumably, felt that the Portuguese would not in practice be able to intervene – and so it was to the Philippines they went, landing in February 1565.

Over the next few years, Legazpi secured the Philippines for Spain, founded Manila and became the new territory's first governor. But Urdaneta's mission was to attempt to return as soon as possible: Philip II had originally instructed, '[they were not to] delay themselves with any trading or rescues, but to immediately return to New Spain, because the principal objective of the journey is to learn the return route, since we already know that the outward voyage is completed in a short time.'[3] Legazpi's 18-year-old grandson, Felipe de Salcedo, was placed in charge of the expedition's lead ship, the *San Pedro*, with Urdaneta plotting the route, and set out in a few weeks.

All previous attempts to sail back across the Pacific had failed. This one succeeded by sailing far north to almost 40°N, rather than trying to avoid the western-blowing trade winds of southern latitudes. The ship arrived in Acapulco in October, having covered more than 13 000 kilometres in 130 days. The *tornaviaje*, or 'return trip', had been accomplished and, more importantly, painstakingly documented by Urdaneta and his deputies, Esteban Rodríguez and Rodrigo Espinosa.

Even at the time, no one was in any doubt about the significance of the achievement. Indeed, Urdaneta was beaten back to New Spain by another ship, captained by Alonso de Arellano, that had arrived two months earlier. Exactly what transpired was and remains unclear, including whether or not Arellano was aware of Urdaneta's plan. Arellano had somehow – and under suspicious circumstances – become separated from Urdaneta's fleet only ten days after the fleet's departure from Mexico and just five days after the true destination had been disclosed at sea to the fleet. Once he had worked his way back, he claimed credit for discovering the *tornaviaje*. But while this claim was being considered by authorities in New Spain, Urdaneta in turn arrived, with the charts and documentation that in the end secured for him the accolades of both his contemporaries and later historians.

For the first time, European ships could reliably sail

the Pacific in both directions. The Polynesians had of course already been covering much of the Pacific for centuries. In our current era of engine-powered ships, to say nothing of aircraft, it can be hard to grasp the notion that travel might be at the mercy of prevailing winds and tides. But up until the advent of steam, one couldn't sail if the wind and sea didn't cooperate, and in much of the ocean, they only cooperated in one direction and at one time of the year.

'Urdaneta's route', as it was soon known, immediately became the basis for the annual deployment of trade vessels known as the Galeón de Manila, or Manila galleons, that sailed the Acapulco–Manila route for the next 250 years. That these were also known as the *nao de China*, or 'China ship', indicates their actual purpose.

Neither Urdaneta nor Legazpi lived long after their respective achievements. Urdaneta died in 1568 in Mexico, while Legazpi died in 1572, only a year after founding Manila. Legazpi left behind a new colony, but one that was itself subordinate to yet another: that of New Spain, based in Mexico. The affairs of a Southeast Asian territory were thus run from Mexico City: the Philippines were seen and treated as the westernmost part of the Americas.

The colony's only real justification was to act as a hub for the Asia, and particularly China, trade. Legazpi reported back to Spain that, 'We are at the gate and in the vicinity of the most fortunate countries of the world, and the most remote; it is three hundred leagues or thereabouts farther than great China, Brunei, Java, Lauzon, Samatra, Maluco, Malaca, Patan, Sian, Lequios, Japan, and other rich and large provinces . . .'[4] Neither Legazpi nor Urdaneta are much remembered outside of specific and specialist histories. Legazpi, the erstwhile governor, has a city named after him, the eponymous Legazpi City, capital of Albay province, located at the base of Mayon volcano and carrying the sobriquet 'City of fun and adventure'. Urdaneta City in Pangasinan, actually a town of 120 000, only dates from the mid-nineteenth century but sports a large, modern monument to Urdaneta in front of the city hall.

*

And what happened to the other party in this Renaissance space race? The Portuguese had never been much interested in the Philippines since the islands seemed to offer nothing of value. Legazpi wrote in a letter in 1569 that 'if his Majesty has an eye only on the Felipina islands, they ought to be considered of little importance, because at present the only article of profit which we can get from this land is cinnamon.'[5] However, the Portuguese were discomfited by the Spaniards being there, and caused such trouble and disruption as they could. Manila complained in 1573 that, 'Last year Chinese vessels came to this city to trade and told us how the Portuguese have asked them not to trade with us, because we were robbers and came to steal and commit other depredations, so that these people wonder not a little if this be true.'[6]

But the crowns of Spain and Portugal were united in 1580, and by the time Portugal regained its independence in 1640, the Portuguese had been largely supplanted in East Asia by the Dutch. Spain emerged, at least for a while, as *'el imperio en el que nunca se pone el sol'*, the empire on which the sun never sets, an empire held together in no small part by the world's first transoceanic shipping lines.

II

The First Transoceanic Shipping Line

'The profits from the China trade have grown
so much, this commerce has so grown, that it
has diminished that in my own realms . . .'

– Philip II, 11 January 1593[1]

Urdaneta's discovery, writes historian Manel Ollé, 'fixed the route of the oldest and most durable shipping line ever established in continuous operation'.[2] The commercial rationale for the project was remembered even on this first voyage, which transported back a small amount of cinnamon – not the most valuable of spices, but a symbolic statement of intent.

Legazpi was however still getting settled. After a few years in Cebu, he moved north to Manila for the better location and harbour. 'We shall gain the commerce with China,' Legazpi wrote as early as 1569, 'whence come silks, porcelains, benzoin, musk, and other articles.'[3] It was not until 1573 that the first galleons left Manila with Chinese trade goods, most notably including a sizeable shipment of silk.

Theodore de Bry 'Navigational vessel of China' (from Latin edition of *Les Grands Voyages*, Frankfurt, 1602), one of the earliest Western depictions of a junk

Trade soon took off: the venerable Filipino historian Benito Legarda, Jr. counted three junks that visited Manila in 1572, six in 1574 and at least a dozen in 1575. By 1580, forty to fifty junks were arriving each year, mainly if not exclusively from the southern province of Fujian. Manila, for its part, was established as a pre-eminent entrepôt, perfectly positioned for collecting silk from China and Japan, the produce of the Spice

Islands to its south and even Indian cotton and Southeast Asian ivory, all for shipment across the Pacific to fill what appeared to be limitless and insatiable demand.[4]

Frontispiece of *Sucesos de las Islas Filipinas* (*Events of the Philippine Islands*) by Antonio de Morga (printed in Mexico, 1609)

The wealth and breadth of the goods on offer from the Chinese were described by lawyer Antonio de Morga in 1609:

> The merchandise that they generally bring and sell to
> the Spaniards consists of raw silk, . . . fine untwisted silk,
> white and of all colors; quantities of velvets, some plain,
> and some embroidered in all sorts of figures, colors, and
> fashions; . . . damasks, satins, . . . and other cloths of all
> colors . . . They also bring musk, benzoin, and ivory; many

bed ornaments, hangings, coverlets, and tapestries of
embroidered velvet; . . . tablecloths, cushions, and
carpets; . . . also some pearls and rubies, sapphires and
crystal-stones; . . . quantities of fine thread of all kinds,
needles, and knick-knacks; little boxes and writing-cases;
beds, tables, chairs, and gilded benches, painted in
many figures and patterns . . . even caged birds, some of
which talk, while others sing, and they make them play
innumerable tricks. The Chinese furnish numberless other
gewgaws and ornaments of little value and worth, which
are esteemed among the Spaniards; besides a quantity of
fine crockery of all kinds; . . . other beads and precious
stones of all colors; pepper and other spices; and rarities
– which, did I refer to them all, I would never finish, nor
have sufficient paper for it.[5]

China trade anecdotes from the period have a ring
of contemporary familiarity. Bishop Domingo Salazar
wrote King Philip in 1590 that:

What has pleased all of us here has been the arrival of a
book-binder from Mexico. He brought books with him,
set up a bindery, and hired a Sangley[6] who had offered
his services to him. The Sangley secretly, and without his
master noticing it, watched how the latter bound books,
and lo, in less than [*blank space*] he left the house, saying
that he wished to serve him no longer, and set up a similar

shop. I assure your Majesty that he became so excellent a workman that his master has been forced to give up the business, because the Sangley has drawn all the trade. His work is so good that there is no need of the Spanish tradesman.[7]

But the Chinese nose for business sometimes misled the visiting merchants. The Jesuit priest Diego de Bobadilla wrote in 1640:

These Chinese merchants are so keen after gain, that, if one sort of merchandise has succeeded well one year, they take a great deal of it the following year. A Spaniard who had lost his nose through a certain illness, sent for a Chinaman to make him one of wood, in order to hide the deformity. The workman made him so good a nose that the Spaniard in great delight paid him munificently, giving him twenty escudos. The Chinaman, attracted by the ease with which he had made that gain, loaded a fine boat-load of wooden noses the next year and returned to Manila. But he found himself very far from his hopes and quite left out in the cold; for, in order to have a sale for that new merchandise, he found that he would have to cut off the noses of all the Spaniards in the country.[8]

*

The Manila galleon would be recognisable today as a shipping line. There were regularly scheduled sailings with specially-built cargo ships. Indeed, for commercial and regulatory reasons – the number of sailings was soon restricted to just one each way per year – the ships grew to become among the largest ever constructed, reaching some 2000 tons, when most large ships were only a quarter of that size; they were the super-container ships of their day.

As a precursor of today's world-leading Asian ship-yards, an entire shipping industry – producing locally-designed ships of locally-supplied materials, constructed and largely crewed by local labour – emerged in Cavite, right outside Manila, to supply the line. The Philippines already had a strong indigenous ship-building tradition, with substantial supplies of local labour augmented by immigrant Chinese artisans. With the sole exception of iron, in which the Philippines was deficient, all other materials, from wood to fabric for sails and rope for rigging, could be supplied locally and from local industry. The galleons' reputation for durability and sturdiness was built upon the local hardwoods: the ships were relatively impervious to both cannon fire and shiprot.[9]

By 1587, single cargoes could be worth as much as 2 million pesos. However, such a huge expansion of trade was not without its problems, a number of which have a distinctly modern sound. One was huge inward migration of Chinese. By 1586, there were 10 000 Chinese in Manila, and despite attempts to control immigration through deportations, the number continued to grow, reaching an estimated 30 000 in 1602.[10] In spite of the mutual profitability of the exercise, tensions would on occasion boil over into violence.

The trade also began untaxed and largely unregulated for a period that corresponded with its initial rapid growth. But there were soon vociferous complaints, largely from Spanish merchants who were losing out to competition, but also from Manileños who were being cut out by Mexican merchants dealing directly. In 1593, the Spanish authorities limited the number of annual sailings on the Acapulco-Manila route to two, and soon after to just one ship in each direction. The amount of trade was also nominally capped to a few hundred thousand pesos, a sum almost always exceeded several times over. American merchants from New Spain were prohibited from dealing with anyone except Manila-based merchants. A second route from Manila to Peru, the other great Spanish colony, was snuffed out after only a few voyages, because the goods they brought competed with Spanish manufactures, particularly Andalusian silk, coming from the other direction. There were many attempts to prohibit intra-American trade of Asian imports as well.

These restrictions could of course never be fully enforced, or much at all. While the freewheeling start of the shipping line became hemmed in by mercantilist regulation and state control, constraints were routinely flouted with false documentation, under-invoicing and outright contraband – practices hardly unknown in the centuries since. Accurate statistics on the trade are consequently hard to come by. The primary constraint on the trade was the physical one of the single ship per year.

By the early 1600s, some 400 people sailed on each ship, some 250 of which were officers, including a silver master responsible for the treasure chests on the way out from New Spain. Other crew included seamen, gunmen and soldiers. The crews were multi-ethnic: only a few of the sailors were Spaniards, while the lower-level crew were largely Filipinos or other Asians.

The voyage was never pleasant and often dangerous: ships could and did sink. Out of the 400 sailings in the 250 years of the Manila galleon, there were fifty-nine shipwrecks.[11] The journey westward from Acapulco to Manila was relatively straightforward, a mere forty-five days if the winds were with the ship, and rarely longer than two months. The typical eastward return trip, however, could take up to six months, putting pressure on provisions and sanitation.

Even if the ship arrived, it was not uncommon for it to do so with fewer people than when it began its journey: the trip was long, provisions were few, scurvy and other diseases common. Giovanni Francesco Gemelli

Careri, an Italian adventurer and traveller, made the trip and described it in his 1699 book *Giro del Mondo*, which appeared in English early in the 1700s:

> There is Hunger, Thirst, Cold, continual Watching, and other Sufferings; besides the terrible Shocks from side to side, caused by the furious beating of the Waves . . .
> [T]he *Galeon* is never clear of an universal raging Itch, as an addition to all other Miseries . . . the Ship swarms with little Vermine, the *Spaniards* called *Gorgojos*, bred in the Bisket; so swift that they in a short time not only run over Cabbins, Beds, and the very Dishes the Men eat on, but insensibly fasten upon the Body . . . There are several other sorts of Vermin of sundry Colours that suck the Blood. Abundance of Flies fall into Dishes of Broth, in which there also swim Worms of several sorts.[12]

It was probably worse for the sailors who could be evicted from their quarters by better-connected passengers.

There was, it seems, some compensation: after complaining about the indigestibility of the dried buffalo meat and the maggots swimming in the broth, Careri notes that, 'during the whole voyage, they never fail of Sweetmeats at Table, and Chocolates twice a Day, of which last the Sailors and Grummets make as great a Consumption, as the richest.'

Sickness prowled the ship due to exposure to 'the

Rains, Cold and other Hardships of the Season', but in spite of:

> The dreadful Sufferings in the prodigious Voyage, yet the desire of Gain prevails with many to venture through it, four, six, and some ten times. The very Sailers, tho' they Forswear the voyage when out at Sea; yet when they come to Acapulco, for the lucre of 275 Pieces of Eight, the King allows them for the Return, never remember past sufferings; like Women after Labour.[13]

The total pay, writes Careri, was 350 of these coins, with only seventy-five paid on the way out. There was some justifiable concern that the Asian sailors might jump ship: 'if they had half, very few would return to the *Philippine Islands* for the rest.' Many stayed anyway, becoming part of the growing Asian immigrant population in New Spain to join, for example, their compatriots making palm wine.

Once was enough for Careri; he vowed never 'to take that Voyage again, which is enough to Destroy a Man, or make him unfit for anything as long as he Lives.'

*

Nevertheless, despite the shipwrecks and terrible conditions, the Manila galleon line lasted for 250 years, with sailings year in and year out. P&O, or rather Peninsular and Oriental Steam Navigation Company, one of the most venerable of modern shipping lines, was, by contrast, founded only in 1837, less than two centuries ago.

The profits were tremendous. Careri estimated that merchants made 150 to 200 per cent; a single cargo could set one up for life. He wrote: 'it is a great Satisfaction to return Home in less than a Year with 17, or 18,000 Pieces of Eight clear Gains, besides a Man's own Venture; a Sum that may make a Man easy as long as he Lives.' The senior officers of the ship, he was told, might clear thousands, indeed tens of thousands, of dollars.

Profits may have kept the Manila galleon going, but its importance to our story is that trade was now, and for the first time, truly global.

III

The Emergence of
the Global Economy

'Although we call them the "Old World" and
the "New World", that's because we only came
across the latter recently, and not because there
are actually two worlds: there is but one.'
– Inca Garcilaso de la Vega, *Comentarios
reales de los incas*, 1609[1]

Once the *tornaviaje* had established itself, voyages
across the Pacific immediately became regular affairs.
The Manila galleon provided the missing link in the
world's global trade network: for the first time, all the
maritime routes – Atlantic, Pacific and Indian Ocean
– were now operational in both directions, knitting
Europe, the Americas, Asia and Africa together.

The Acapulco–Manila line itself formed part of a
much longer single route of some 24 000 kilometres
that connected Seville with Manila under a single gov-
erning jurisdiction: the *Casa de Contratación*, or 'House

of Trade', in Seville. Asian silk, porcelain, ivory and spices would be sent across the Pacific from Manila to Acapulco. In these pre-Panama Canal days, goods had to cross the isthmus overland. The route – it might be too much to call it a 'road' (it was unpaved with mules providing most of the transport) – from Acapulco to Mexico City was known as the 'Camino de China'. From Mexico City, goods continued to the Caribbean port of Veracruz, where they were loaded on the *Flota de Indias* – the West Indies Fleet – which sailed to Seville. Havana served as a transhipment hub. Goods such as wine, oil and manufactured products would go in the other direction.

Acapulco, its fine harbour notwithstanding, had little to recommend it. 'As for the City of *Acapulco*,' wrote world traveller Gemelli Careri, 'I think it might more properly be call'd a poor Village of Fishermen, than the chief Mart of the South Sea, and Port for the Voyage to China; so mean and wretched are the Houses being made of nothing but Wood, Mud and Straw.'[2]

The arrival of the Manila galleon in Acapulco occasioned a huge annual trade fair, during which the population swelled by thousands. Careri went on to observe that:

Most of the Officers and Merchants that came aboard the *Peru* Ships, went to lie ashore, bringing with them two

Aquapolque (Acapulco) by Nicolaes van Geelkercken, engraving, from
East and West Indian Mirror (1619)

> Millions of Pieces of Eight to lay out in Commodities of
> *China*; so that . . . *Acapulco* was converted from a rustick
> village into a populous City; . . . to which was added .
> . . a great concourse of Merchants from *Mexico*, with
> abundance of Pieces of Eight and Commodities of the
> Country and of *Europe*.[3]

Alexander von Humboldt noted in his *Political Essay
on the Kingdom of New Spain* that when he visited in
1803, it was still 'the most renowned trade fair in the
whole world'. [4]

*

'[T]hese wares are so cheap that their
like cannot be supplied from Spain.'
– Juan Grau y Monfalcón, 1637[5]

Unlike earlier centuries, and perhaps not since the
Roman Empire, international trade now affected the
consumption of relatively ordinary people. Textiles
made up the bulk of goods imported into Mexico.
These were not just silk, and not just fabric: they also
included finished items such as clothing, bed linens
and rugs. These were the mass-market consumer goods
of the age, which city-dwellers came to expect and
rural populations desired. Everyone, it seemed, from
the indigenous peoples now forced by Spanish con-
vention and law to wear clothing, to sophisticated city-
dwellers, went about in garments made from Asian
silks and cottons. Asian, and mostly Chinese-sup-
plied, consumer goods that were once luxuries became
necessities.

*

By a century or so into the Manila galleon, Manila
merchants offered a wide range of cottons from India's
Coromandel Coast, including calicoes, chitas, cam-
bays and ginghams.[6] Manila wasn't just an entrepôt for
China anymore.

Silk manufacturing in China, from Jean-Baptiste du Halde, *Description Geographique de l'empire de la chine*, vol. 2, p. 217 (1736)

The porcelain trade offers particular examples of the increasingly global nature of commerce. Chinese manufacturers developed new products for the American market, the consumption of chocolate providing a notable illustration. Based on local indigenous practice, chocolate was drunk from coconut shells or gourds known as *jícaras*, which later in the colonial period were kept upright in silver mounts called *mancerinas*. Both *jícaras* and *mancerinas* were soon redesigned in porcelain for American and European markets by Chinese manufacturers in Jingdezhen, where porcelain production increasingly took on industrial characteristics as factories expanded in size and complexity.[7] Mexico's main domestic pottery industry in Puebla, meanwhile, emulated the Chinese blue and white style as well as several of the Chinese forms, such as double gourds and high-shouldered vases.[8] Shards of broken porcelain, known as *chinitas*, were also used as small coinage.

The economy of New Spain became dependent on the Asian trade. In 1637, Juan Grau y Monfalcón, procurator-general for Manila, wrote to King Philip IV that, 'the trade of the Philippines is so necessary today in New Spain, that the latter country finds it as difficult as do the islands to get along without that trade.'[9]

Trade supported local industry. Grau y Monfalcón noted that raw silk imports provided raw material for 14 000 Mexican weavers, while imported Asian cottons, 'are so cheap that their like cannot be supplied from Spain . . . For the Indians and blacks care only for the linens of China and the Philippines, and, if they do not have them, they get along without them . . .'[10] To counter what would today be called 'protectionism', he argued that cheap Asian cloth was even necessary to the operation of the ever-important mines:

Consequently, with one thousand pesos' worth of it they maintained their mining operations longer than they could

with five thousand worth of that from Spain. From that
it follows that if [the supply of] it were to fail, the mines
would necessarily decrease; and that would redound to
the greater damage of the royal treasury, and to that of the
country, your vassals, and commerce . . .[11]

This trade in industrial goods integrating the two economies also went beyond textiles. China served as a source
of the mercury used in the extraction of the silver, which
underlaid the entire trade. Although the most important
source of mercury was in the Peruvian town of Huan-
cavelica, attempts were made to import it from China
via Manila. Humboldt reported that it was found to be
impure, with high levels of lead.[12]

Trade goods and their influence extended beyond
the Americas. Much of the silk, porcelain and spices
that entered Acapulco found its way to Spain. But a
particularly illustrative example is the famous and still
immensely popular Manila shawl (*mantón de Manila*), a
square piece of fringed silk lavishly and vividly embroidered with flowers, birds and other images. This staple of
Spanish fashion has its origins in Guangdong. Its name
reflects the route it took.

Commercial integration extended to people as well
as goods. In 1635, Spanish barbers (who engaged in
bloodletting as well as haircutting and were thus a sort
of medical practitioner) in Mexico City complained to

the municipal council of unfair competition from Chinese barbers. The council sided with the complainants and recommended that the Chinese barbershops be limited to twelve and be relegated to the suburbs.[13] In 1667, there were, however, more than 100 (mostly unlicensed) Asian barbershops operating within Mexico City.

Asian immigrants were also active in various other professions. The early seventeenth century visitor and prelate Thomas Gage noted that, 'The goldsmiths' shops and works are to be admired, the Indians and the people of China that have been made Christians and every year come thither, have perfected the Spaniards in that trade.'[14]

The flow of people was largely unidirectional: Chinese merchants went to Manila, but Spanish merchants rarely returned the favour, nor did China allow it; Chinese and Filipinos went to the Americas in inestimable thousands, while Spaniards went to Manila in hundreds and thousands and to China – even including missionaries – in perhaps dozens. Furthermore, this international trade played a far greater proportional role in the Americas and the Philippines – given that it was Manila's sole reason for existence – than it did in China, whose economy was much larger and more diversified.

Influence nevertheless went in both directions. China could not help but be affected by the increased commercial activity. Demand for goods drove not just manufacturing in China, but the export-oriented manufacturing sector in particular that was to stand China in good stead in the next few centuries. More significantly, China was transformed by crops introduced from the New World as part of what has come to be known as the 'Columbian Exchange'. These new crops arrived more by agricultural diffusion than by the sort of commercial trade that was the Manila galleon's primary *raison-d'être*. The money may have been in Asian cash crops like spices and tea, but maize, sweet potatoes and peanuts – which could be grown in previously marginally arable land – allowed the Chinese population growth to spike upwards in the eighteenth century.

There had of course been movements of goods, people, crops and ideas before, some even transformative. But never between all the continents, and never on this scale. And because of the asymmetry in the trade and migration patterns, the centre of all this movement and mixing was not Canton, Beijing, Madrid, London or even Constantinople; it was instead Mexico City, the very place whose people, upon the successful return of Urdaneta from the Philippines, came to 'believe that they will be the center of the world'.[15]

IV

The First World City

'those of Mexico . . . believe that they
will be the center of the world.'
– Spanish letter about the discovery
of the *tornaviaje*, 1566[1]

Several cities today, notably London, New York and Hong Kong, have claims to being a 'world city', a place where people, goods and ideas meet, with money an essential accelerant; many others aspire to the status.

But the first world city was none of these: it was Mexico City. Indeed, for two centuries, Mexico was arguably the centre of the world, the place where Asia, Europe and the Americas all met, and where people intermingled and exchanged everything from genes to textiles.

Even before the advent of the Manila galleon trade, New Spain was immensely rich from the wealth of the conquered indigenous peoples. Bishop-elect Juan de Zumárraga wrote to Charles V in 1529 that, 'Silks are so common here that mechanics and servants of people of the lower classes, and women of the same, and mistresses and spinsters go about covered with silks, capes and smocks and skirts and kerchiefs . . .'[2]

The silks referred to by Zumárraga in his letter were probably locally-produced: sericulture had been introduced to Mexico from Spain by Hernán Cortés. Raw silk from China via the Manila galleon replaced local Mexican silk, one of the economic dislocations caused by Asian competition.

It was this wealth in the Americas, rather than just the markets back in Europe, that provided the economic impetus for the galleon trade and kept it going for two and a half centuries. In 1610, the poet Bernardo de Balbuena, who hailed from Mexico, in a work grandiloquently entitled *La Grandeza Mexicana* (*The Grandeur of Mexico City*) described it as 'the richest and most opulent city, with the most trade and the most treasure . . .'[3]

Visitors remarked on the extravagance. Thomas Gage, who had travelled through Mexico in 1625, wrote disparagingly of what he saw as an ostentatious luxury, 'Both men and women are excessive in their apparel, using more silks than stuffs and cloths; precious stones and pearls further much this their vain ostentation; a hatband and rose, made of diamonds, in a gentleman's hat, is common, and a hatband of pearls is ordinary in a tradesman.'[4] He noted the city's wide streets and innumerable coaches, some of which, 'exceed the cost of the best of the court of Madrid and other parts of Christendom; for there they spare no silver, nor gold, nor precious stones, nor cloth of gold, nor the best silks of China to enrich them.' Marvelling at the opulence of religious establishments, Gage observed:

> There is in the cloister of the Dominicans a lamp hanging
> in the church, with 300 branches made of silver, to hold so
> many candles, beside 100 little lamps for oil set in it, every
> one being made of several workmanship, so exquisitely,
> that it is valued at four hundred thousand ducats; and with
> such like curious works are many streets made more rich
> and beautiful by the shops of goldsmiths . . .[5]

These were the same goldsmiths presumably staffed, as he said, by 'the Indians and the people of China'.

However, commerce did not lead merely to ostentation. Inexpensive textiles, as we have seen, were crucial to the economy. Yet another result was a convergence of different sorts of cosmopolitanism and sophistication. Chocolate, for example, the first of several hot drinks to conquer the world and define modern leisure consumption, was – being a Mexican drink to begin with – developed in the Americas before being introduced to Europe. And chocolate was drunk, as we have already noted, from Chinese porcelain copies of indigenous American drinking vessels.

*

By the 1540s, three decades before the arrival of the first galleons from Asia, Mexico City was already one of the richest cities in the world, but it was a cultural and intellectual centre as well. Boasting a printing press as early as 1535, and universities decades before any of its North American counterparts, it was a city of books, writers and students, providing fertile ground for the intellectual and cultural input from Asia later in the century.

Juan González de Mendoza conducted the research for his history of China, *Historia de las cosas más notables, ritos y costumbres del gran reyno de la China*[6] (published in Rome in 1585), in Mexico, where he interviewed trans-Pacific travellers. Translated into several languages, this was the first bestseller on China, and remained one for decades. Mexico's own printing presses turned out original works such as Antonio de Morga's *Sucesos de las Islas Filipinas (Events in the Philippine Islands)*, published in Mexico in 1609, a firsthand account of Spanish relations with China, Japan and Southeast Asia, which remains an important reference for understanding the region at the turn of the century.[7]

In Sor Juana Inés de la Cruz, seventeenth century Mexico produced a world-class poet and one of the first feminists to boot:

Hombres necios que acusáis

    You foolish men who lay

a la mujer sin razón,

    the guilt on women,

sin ver que sois la ocasión

    not seeing you're the cause

de lo mismo que culpáis . . .

    of the very thing you blame . . .[8]

*

When Asians started arriving in Mexico – almost as soon as the Acapulco–Manila line started running – it was already a multicultural, cosmopolitan place. During the period of the Manila galleon, 40 000 to 60 000 and perhaps as many as 100 000 Asians – mostly Chinese and, in particular Filipinos – passed through Acapulco to settle in New Spain. The majority were sailors; by the early 1600s, most of the sailors on the Pacific route were East Asians. Some came as servants and some, unfortunately, came as slaves. The list of occupations of these early Asian migrants included barbers, vendors of imported goods, harp players, dancers, scribes, tailors, cobblers, silversmiths and coachmen.[9]

In Mexico City's Plaza Mayor, known today as Zócalo, there was an outdoor marketplace of stalls and shops called the Parián after the Chinese district in Manila.

In this market Asian vendors mixed with those from the world over. The Parián became a permanent edifice at the turn of the eighteenth century, while the term *parián* became the word for 'marketplace' in many cities of Mexico.

The poet Bernardo de Balbuena said that, in Mexico, 'the best of all the world, the cream of what is known and produced, here abounds, is sold and cheap'[10]; he listed spices from Southeast Asia, ivory, diamonds, Chinese porcelain, Indian fabrics, Siamese ebony and rubies and emeralds from India and Ceylon.

Asian influence entered the arts and products of the New World. Chinese blue and white porcelain was, as we have seen, extensively emulated. Japanese lacquer desks and Chinese wall-hangings were copied and adapted locally. The sixteenth Viceroy, Lope Díez de Armendáriz at some point between 1635 and 1640 received a folding screen called a *biombo* in Spanish, the word derived from the Japanese *byōbu*. This particular example has panels painted in traditional European style showing some of Mexico City's best-known spots, such as the Plaza Mayor or Zócalo, with however very Japanese-looking gilt scroll clouds. Furthermore, a Mexican painting technique called *enconchado*, typified by a painted over mother-of-pearl, developed as a fusion of pre-Columbian and perhaps Asian shell inlay, European oils and Japanese lacquer.

Balbuena, all the way back in 1610, described his city in what must still stand today as the definition of a 'world city': 'In you, Spain joins with China, Italy with Japan, and finally the whole world in commerce and order . . .'[11]

*

While Manila did not approach Mexico City in urbanisation or sophistication, and so perhaps did not qualify as a 'world city', its role at the Asian terminus of the Manila galleon meant that it rapidly developed into a regional trading hub. Although trade with Chinese merchants dominated, ships from around Asia, and as far away as India, also anchored in Manila.

Manila was, in terms of population, very much a Chinese city. The Chinese (or *Sangleyes* as they were known) constituted the commercial core of the city, even while they were confined to the *Parián* – beginning a pattern of urban sinicisation that was to repeat itself throughout Southeast Asia. In his account of his trip around the world, Careri wrote: 'Within a Musket Shot of the Gate of Parian, is the Habitation of the Chinese merchants called *Sangley*, who in several Streets have rich Shops of Silk, Purcellane, and other Commodities. Here are found all the Arts and Trade, so that all the Citizens are worth, runs through their Hands, through the fault of the Spaniards and Indians, who apply themselves to nothing.'[12]

Manila played a key role in the dissemination of information about China. Martín de Rada, who had sailed with the Legazpi expedition, acquired the first Western library of Chinese books as early as 1575. His accounts provided much of the material for Mendoza's history. The first translation of a classical Chinese text into a European language also took place in Manila: the *Mingxin baojian*, rendered by Juan Cobo as *Espejo rico del claro corazón*.[13] The translation was published in Manila in 1593, and was printed, interestingly enough, using the Chinese method of woodblocks.[14] Cobo also translated Seneca into Chinese. The University of Santo Tomas, founded in 1611, more than two decades before Harvard, is the oldest continuously operating university in the Philippines.

It was hardly smooth sailing. The Spanish presence was numerically small and outnumbered not only by Filipinos but by the new immigrant Chinese community. While the various ethnic communities – Spanish, Filipino, Chinese, Japanese – coexisted, ethnic friction and perceived existential threats could boil over with disastrously fatal consequences. Many thousands of Chinese were killed in the infamous 1603 massacre. But, in spite of being largely illegal under Chinese law, the lure of trade was irresistible, and the numbers of

Chinese residents nevertheless soon rebounded.

Manila, as curious as it must seem today, was subordinate to Mexico rather than Spain until the end of the eighteenth century. This, in effect, gave American Mexico an Asian province while simultaneously engendering early Asian links with the New World that were, in terms of population flows, larger than those with Europe. One peculiar result of these relationships and Spanish control of the Pacific was to put Mexico closer to the cutting edge of international diplomacy than a colony otherwise would have been. In 1613, the Japanese diplomatic mission of Hasekura Tsunenaga went first to New Spain before proceeding to Europe. After meeting the emperor and pope, and converting to Catholicism, the mission returned to Japan by the same route in 1619.

Another peculiar result of the Spain-Mexico-Manila axis was the rise of world's first currency in common and accepted use across multiple continents. Pre-dating both the pound and the greenback, it was a currency emanating from Mexico. Minted in the Americas, Spanish milled dollars became the currency of choice throughout most of East Asia.

V

A Global Currency

'[Silver] is the most valuable article in the Acapulco
ships which sail to Manila. The silver of the new
continent seems in this manner to be one of the principal
commodities by which the commerce between the
two extremities of the old one is carried on, and it is
by means of it, in a great measure, that those distant
parts of the world are connected with one another.'
— Adam Smith, *The Wealth of Nations*[1]

There are two sides to every trade. But the Spaniards
hankering for the riches of China ran across an immedi-
ate problem: China had little interest in outside goods.
Don Martín Enríquez, the viceroy in Mexico, wrote the
King in December 1570, just after the first round trips
across the Pacific:

And one of the difficulties consequent upon this commerce and intercourse is, that neither from this land nor
from Spain, so far as can now be learned, can anything be

49

exported thither which they do not already possess. They have an abundance of silks, and linen likewise, according to report. Cloths, on account of the heat prevalent in the country, they never use nor value. Wax, drugs, and cotton are super-abundant in the islands, whither the Chinese go to obtain them by barter.[2]

There was, however, one thing the Chinese would accept: 'And thus, to make a long story short, the commerce with that land must be carried on with silver, which they value above all other things; and I am uncertain whether your Majesty will consent to this on account of having to send it to a foreign kingdom.'[3]

Silver nevertheless became the main commodity of the Manila galleon trade, a situation continually ago-nised over and sometimes regretted in the decades and centuries to come. But whether measured in the many tens of tons or several millions of pesos, a staggering amount of silver passed annually from the Americas into the Chinese money supply. Silver was so central to the developments of this period that the trans-Pacific trade route that we have called it *la ruta de la plata* – a silver, rather than silk, road that changed the global economy forever.

Silver had come to dominate the Chinese economy by the sixteenth century. Paper money, which China pioneered, had all but collapsed in value due to rampant overprinting, requiring a return to metallic coinage. Gold coins came in denominations too large for ordinary transactions, while copper coins came with their own problems: silver coins can be assayed for purity, but the only way to test a copper coin was to melt it down, which rather defeated the purpose of having coins in the first place. Copper coins also came in multiple varieties of weights and metal content, which made transactions onerous. Silver was just simpler.[4]

By the late sixteenth century, the Ming Dynasty had consolidated all taxes into payments in silver – the Single-Whip system – even for peasants, who were no longer permitted to pay in kind.[5] The Chinese money supply, serving more than a quarter of the world's population, had been standardised on silver. China, however, had limited available silver of its own, and while considerable amounts came – via Portuguese intermediaries, as it turns out – from mines in Japan, these evidently did not suffice.

Spain's colonies in America did, however, have supplies of silver that could at times seem unlimited.

*

Soy el rico Potosí, del mundo soy el tesoro;

soy el rey de los montes, envidia soy de los reyes'

('I am rich Potosí, the treasure of the world;

the king of mountains, the envy of kings').

— From the inscription on Potosí's coat-of-arms,

bestowed by Emperor Charles V[6]

Juan Niño de Tabora, governor of the Philippines, wrote of the Chinese to the King in 1628 that, 'their god is silver, and their religion the various ways that they have of gaining it'.[7] If that were so, the Chinese god lived up a mountain in the high Andes.

In 1545, the great silver mine at Potosí was discovered at 4000 metres in what is now Bolivia. It soon became the single largest source of silver in the world, at times producing more than half the world's silver. Within a few decades, Potosí had a population larger than any other city in the Americas, equivalent to that of Paris or London. 'This would be the modern-day equivalent of, say, 20 million people moving to a spot on Alaska's North Slope,' write Flynn and Giraldez.[8]

The initial inscription was updated to: '*Para el poderoso Emperador, para el sabio Rey, este excelso monte de plata conquistará el mundo.*'[9] ('For the powerful Emperor, for the wise King, this lofty mountain of silver will conquer the world.') Potosí is referenced in Don Quixote; Matteo Ricci placed it on his Chinese world map in 1602. By the end of the sixteenth century, Potosí boasted three dozen casinos, more than a dozen dance halls, eighty churches and fountains with wine and *chicha*, Andean corn beer.[10]

Theodore de Bry, miners in Potosí, engraving (1590)

This was mining on an industrial scale, augmented by one of history's more important – but certainly unhealthy – industrial innovations: the use of mercury rather than smelting to extract the silver from the ore, thus making lower-grade ores economical and extending the life of the mine. That this silver amalgamation process was invented in Mexico in the mid-sixteenth century is another indication of the general level of sophistication, intellectual and otherwise, that could be found in Spanish America.

The resources – the actual metal – technically belonged to the Crown, but the mining itself was outsourced for a one-fifth royalty, or quinta. The balance, less the cost of production (relatively low, thanks to silver amalgamation) remained as profit, explaining the wealth and purchasing power in the colonies: there was a lot of money looking for things to buy. And it found them in Asia via the Manila galleon.

The numbers are staggering: by far the bulk of the world's silver emanated from Spanish America, and of that amount, about a third (other estimates are higher[11]) ended up directly or indirectly in China.

The economics of these silver-for-silks transactions have been much written about, but there are some additional aspects worth considering. Silver, although a commodity, is also a currency. So while it is true that the silverisation of the Chinese economy resulted in the price of silver soaring, the question remains: relative to what? A dollar is always, by definition, worth a dollar, and an ounce of silver is always worth an ounce of silver.

A merchant by the name of Pedro de Baeza provided an explanation in 1609: 'For as much as throughout all the kingdom of China there is an enormous quantity of fine gold of more than twenty-two carats touch; if this were brought to New Spain, or to Castile, a profit of 75 to 80 per cent would be made on the price as between one region and the other.'[12] He is advocating what today we might call exchange rate arbitrage: profiting from the different rates of exchanges that prevail in different markets. He further explains:

> [Gold] is regarded in China as a commodity which rises and falls in accordance with the supply and the demand, and it does not have a fixed value there as here in Castile. A peso of gold in China is often worth 5 ½ pesos of silver, and if there is a shortage thereof and a demand for it elsewhere, the rate may rise to six or 6 ½ silver pesos for one of gold. The dearest at which I have ever bought it or seen it sold in the city of Canton in China, was 7 ½ silver pesos for one of gold, and I never saw it go higher, nor has it done so hitherto. Whereas in Spain a peso of gold is usually worth 12 ½ silver pesos, whereby it can be seen how more than 75 to 80 per cent can be gained on gold which is exported from China.[13]

In other words, priced in gold, silver was worth relatively more in China than in Spain. One might then expect gold to flow out of China as silver flowed in, and this is what happened.[14]

The great eighteenth century economist, Adam Smith, took note of exactly this in *The Wealth of Nations*, published in 1776, towards the end of the galleon period:

. . . in the East Indies, particularly in China and Indostan,
the value of the precious metals, when the Europeans
first began to trade to those countries, was much higher
than in Europe; and it still continues to be so . . . It is
more advantageous, too, to carry silver thither than gold;
because in China, and the greater part of the other markets
of India, the proportion between fine silver and fine gold is
but as ten, or at most as twelve to one; whereas in Europe
it is as fourteen or fifteen to one. In China, and the greater
part of the other markets of India, ten, or at most twelve
ounces of silver, will purchase an ounce of gold; in Europe,
it requires from fourteen to fifteen ounces.[15]

The inverse is that Asian goods were worth a lot more
silver once exported to the Americas than they were
back in Asia. The abundance of silver did not itself
make it cheap for merchants; while the cost of capital (that is, the interest rate if they had to borrow it)
might have been lower than if capital were not so
plentiful, merchants nevertheless would have paid a
peso for every peso. Their profit could only come from
direct silver-gold arbitrage above – or, since the traders
were on the whole merchants rather than bankers,
channelling the transactions through goods.

Arbitrage opportunities occur when there are economic imbalances; arbitrage itself tends to correct those
imbalances. By 1635, the silver-gold exchange rate in

China had collapsed to approximately the rate previously reported for Spain, greatly reducing or eliminating the profits from mining.

The world's financial markets were now, for the first time, global. Up until the sixteenth century, the financial links between the continents had a lot of play in them: there was little mechanism to transmit what today would be called contagion. Potosí changed that, first by delivering what must have seemed like a limitless supply of bullion to the Spanish Crown, and then into the economy as a whole. With the *tornaviaje* and the direct access to the differential silver-gold exchange rates of China, the value of that silver doubled almost overnight.

Money supplies were also now global rather than just regional. Relative prices that were out of sync with world averages tended to be arbitraged away, directly or through trade, while inflation or other economic problems were no longer constrained to a single economy. China's move to a silver-based economy affected the economic trajectory of Europe. The primary link was the Manila galleon.

All of this came from a single ship, albeit a very large one, in each direction every year: as improbable as that may seem, populations and economies – and hence trade – were a great deal smaller four centuries ago. Spain, for example, had a population of just 7 million, smaller even than the population of Hong Kong today.

Two thousand tons of cargo in one direction and a few million pesos of silver in the other could and did create and move markets.

Some of the first visible consequences arose a few decades into the sixteenth century. Because the actual supply of silver was almost entirely outside China's control – as if the United States used, say, oil for money – the Chinese money supply was in danger of sharp contractions from external shocks. Starting in 1638, three galleons were lost in succession, with both goods and silver going to the bottom of the sea. Potosí was going through a bad patch. Japanese restrictions on trade with Europeans, starting in 1635, also greatly curtailed the other great source of silver.[16] Considerable effort has been made over the years to quantify the inflows of silver to China; inflows are however, not the same as the money supply itself, which is at least to some extent cumulative. Money supply is therefore a difficult number to measure. Nevertheless, a sharp cut in imports must have constrained the money supply, the economy and the ability to pay taxes. While cause and effect remain inconclusive, the Ming Dynasty fell in the next decade.

Spain, meanwhile, was affected by the diminished profitability of silver extraction. Due to the inflation caused by previous decades of increased supply, the silver they had lost its buying power. It was precisely in the early 1640s that Spain suffered the first decisive military and political defeats, resulting in withdrawing from a major role in European affairs.

Then as today, the West – Europe and the Americas – minted money, which it sent to China in exchange for consumer goods. China manufactured and the West consumed. The results this engendered sound familiar: Western domestic industry was undercut by imports, money was spent on consumption rather than investment, increases in the money supply led to inflation. The Chinese economy, meanwhile, became subject to financial shocks outside its control. But if China had not acted as a sink for the American-sourced silver, even more of it would surely have ended up in Europe, possibly resulting in economic and political distortions even greater than those Spain experienced as it was.

Something of a pause set in in the mid-1600s, as China worked through the political and economic difficulties surrounding the fall of the Ming Dynasty and accession of the Qing. Spain's tendency to overextend itself in European military adventures had also finally caught up with it. But a second silver boom picked up in the eighteenth century. Chinese population growth had increased due to the new crops introduced from America, and the increased demand caused silver prices to spike again relative to gold. Demand was met this time mostly from Mexican mines; more silver was produced in Spanish America in the eighteenth century than in the previous two centuries combined. By mid-century, the silver-gold rate had returned to balance.[17]

But this later period of eighteenth century expansion coincided with a significant financial innovation: the introduction of the 'milled' Spanish dollar. There had already been 'Spanish dollars' before this. The term actually derives from the German *thaler*, a coin dating from the early sixteenth century. Equivalents, known as *real de a ocho* or *peso de ocho* (whence 'pieces of eight') were minted in Spain and the New World from the sixteenth century. Each was worth eight reales, a different denomination of 3.44 grams of silver.

'Cob' 8 reales, Philip III (Mexico, 1610)

Mexico had had a mint since 1536. Minting was, at that time, a largely manual process. *Macuquinas*, or 'cobs', were made by cutting a silver bar into pieces of the appropriate weight and then striking a design onto them with a hammer and die. The cobs' irregular shape made them susceptible to clipping – a common practice.

Charles III 'pillar dollar'
(Mexico, 1771)

But in the 1730s, coins were introduced whose blanks were made on a milling machine to ensure a consistent weight and size. Their edges were also raised with serrated edges, meaning that it was easy to tell if metal had been shaved or clipped off. These coins, known as *real fuerte columnario, columnarios de mundos y mares* or 'pillar dollars' were minted in Mexico City from 1732 to 1772, at which point Charles III decreed that the coins must show his portrait. Their name derives from the original design of two globes – representing the Old and New Worlds – between pillars, under a crown.

Charles IIII portrait
dollar (Mexico, 1798);
note the IIII (i.e. four
character or *sigong*)

As a result of their regularity and security features, these coins became the most widely accepted currency in the world and, indeed, the first to approach universal acceptance. The portrait coins were nicknamed 'head dollars' (*fanmian*) in Chinese. The coins of Charles III and Charles IV (or IIII) were known as *sangong* and *sigong* (three-character and four-character) coins respectively.[18] They were also known by the Chinese as 'Buddha heads' (*foutou*) due to the perceived resemblance of the busts of the Spanish monarchs to images of the Buddha.

China, curiously, seems not to have minted silver coins. Ingots, measured by the *tael*, varied from place to place and from trade to trade, making it a clumsy medium of exchange. As a result, Spanish dollar coins progressively competed with and replaced the *tael*: standardised coinage facilitated trade. Many examples of Spanish dollars can be seen today with Chinese chops or assay marks.

The Manila galleon came to an end in 1815 with the advent of the Mexican War of Independence. But the coin lived on. In the 1850s, the Mexican 'eagle' dollar was formally accepted as a substitute. Various 'trade dollars' sprang up, including the French Indochinese *piastre*, using the same specification. The yuan and yen are both direct descendants; both mean 'round', as the coin was. Even the British did not use the pound in Hong Kong, but instead introduced the Hong Kong dollar on the same model. The name for the Malaysian version, the ringgit, is an old Malay word meaning 'jagged', and refers to the Spanish dollars' serrated edges.

Even the US dollar derived from the same coin, which was, in fact, legal tender until the mid-nineteenth century. The expression 'two bits' for twenty-five cents comes from the old 'piece of eight'. Stocks in the United States were priced in one-eighth-dollar increments until the end of the twentieth century.

The US dollar and the Chinese yuan are cousins if not siblings. Both are descendants of the eighteenth century Spanish milled dollar. So if, as some commentators speculate, the Chinese yuan ends up replacing the US dollar as the world's reserve currency, then – in some ways – nothing very much will have changed.

VI

The Birth Of
Globalisation

The key element in the term 'globalisation' is 'global'. Not only were critical elements of globalisation in place by the early modern period, but we can date its inception exactly. Whatever processes of internationalisation and integration might have been underway before 1565 and Urdaneta's *tornaviaje*, they were regional rather than global in scope. According to Dennis O. Flynn and Arturo Giráldez:

> Global trade emerged when 1) all heavily populated
> continents began to exchange products continuously—
> both with each other directly and indirectly via other
> continents—and 2) the value of the goods exchanged
> became sufficient to generate lasting impacts on all trading
> partners. It is true that important intercontinental trade
> existed prior to the 16th century, but there was no direct

trade link between America and Asia before the founding of Manila as a Spanish entrepôt in 1571. Prior to that year, the world market was not yet fully coherent or complete; after that year it was.[1]

That the world was a very different place in 1566 than it was in 1564 is clearly shown by how quickly the Manila galleon trade developed: there were regular commercial sailings within a decade. If, as Flynn and Giráldez do, one puts the actual start date a few years later at 1571–73 (giving Legazpi time to found Manila and send an actual Chinese cargo to Acapulco), then the ramping up happened with a speed that would seem enviable even today. From inception to execution, the new shipping line took less time than the Transcontinental railroad, the Trans-Siberian railroad, the Suez or Panama Canals or even the Internet.

Each of the elements that characterise globalisation – global trade networks, shipping lines, integrated financial markets, flows of cultures and peoples – can be found in the late sixteenth and early seventeenth centuries. A global currency based around the Spanish 'dollar' predated the US dollar's similar role by two centuries. The attributes of today's world cities typified Mexico 400 years ago.

Globalisation itself, therefore, evidently predates everything that conventional (Anglo-American) wisdom holds necessary for it: the Enlightenment, steam, free trade, laissez-faire capitalism, liberal political systems and the more recent, Western-initiated multinational institutions as such more recent the World Bank and IMF. Whatever it is that sparks and sustains globalisation cannot be linked to this particular narrative, for the basic structures of globalisation existed at least two centuries before any of these developments took root.

Globalisation is a matter of degree, not a binary. But it was during the decidedly Spanish-dominated decades straddling the turn of the sixteenth century that humanity's activities first reached global scale.

This was when the first trade networks united Asia, Europe, the Americas, as well as, it should be added, Africa, with uninterrupted commercial shipping. It was also the period when the world's financial markets first became linked through the medium of silver. A century or so later, but well within the Manila galleon period, the world's first global currency emerged in the form of the milled Spanish silver dollar that in turn begat currencies in countries from the United States to China and Japan.

These networks and interactions were not nearly as sophisticated or integrated as those today, nor were they as fast. After all, the news that Portugal had succeeded in regaining independence from the Spanish crown in December 1640 didn't reach Macau until 31 May 1642

– much slower than the Internet even on a very bad day. But from 1565 on, what happened in China no longer just stayed in China. In a single sentence in 1609, Pedro de Baeza discusses currency markets in China, Europe and the Americas.[2] Before 1565, the discovery of a mountain of silver only affected China once the metal travelled through the markets of Europe, the Levant, India and elsewhere. After 1565, ingots and coins could be placed in a ship and reach China within months, with minimal intermediaries and mark-ups. It was not quite a telegraphic transfer, but neither was it a process of slow diffusion via indirect trade.

Nor were these early-modern networks the result, as today's are, of deliberate government policy. Indeed, many if not most of the Chinese and Spanish traders were operating contrary to laws and regulations promulgated by their respective emperors: globalisation took root in spite of concerted official efforts to prevent it. Globalisation, had anyone stopped to think about it, was hardly a foregone conclusion, however inevitable it looks today. The historian Manel Ollé makes the point that Sino-Spanish interactions in the sixteenth century were an ambivalent process, intensively commercial but socially and institutionally unstable.[3]

Despite the uncertainty, however, globalisation had then the effects one might have expected. In China, overseas demand drove manufacturing and economic growth, which in turn supported the population growth made possible by the innovation in new crops. Financial integration created arbitrage opportunities, which led to more efficient allocation of financial resources; this integration in turn allowed contagion from one economy to another, such as the economic shocks of ship sinkings – a single sinking would knock out a year's trade.

The Manila galleons sailed for two and a half centuries, until 1815 and the dawn of a new era of independence for most of Spanish America. The world was during this period a very different place from the one it would later become.

China had the largest, most productive and most dynamic economy in the world. Even a couple of centuries later, Adam Smith would still write in *The Wealth of Nations*: 'China is a much richer country than any part of Europe, and the difference between the price of subsistence in China and in Europe is very great. Rice in China is much cheaper than wheat is anywhere in Europe.'[4]

China was and still is the factory to the world. During the Manila galleon trade, however, Chinese products were competing not just on price but also on their unsurpassed quality. Consumer-product innovation was mostly an East Asian and largely Chinese monopoly: it was manufacturers in the West – Mexico and then Europe – that copied Asian silks, porcelain, screens, fans and furniture – not the other way around.

The China of the sixteenth century looked to the West not for development or investment, but rather for the silver needed for the Chinese money supply.

China was not just the most economically developed country in the world, it was also the most powerful. Unlike the 1840s, when British ships could force their way up the Pearl River and require China to buy opium, gunboat commerce was not a practical option for the early-modern Europeans in the region.

Combining force with commerce was successful only in the Southeast Asian periphery where, for example, it was Dutch East India Company policy – according to the company's Governor-General in 1614 – that 'trade cannot be maintained without war'.[5] But none of Spain, Portugal or Holland was able to project much force against large, long-standing nations in East Asia. They managed at best only politically insignificant footholds on the coasts of China and Japan, whence they were always in danger of being expelled. China was able to require that trade take place on its own terms, restricted to certain ports and times.

In Japan, after decades of religious conflict, the Tokugawa rulers decided to expel the Portuguese and closed their borders, except to the Dutch, whom they restricted to the small man-made island of Dejima in 1640, a situation which lasted for more than two centuries until Commodore Perry appeared with his Black

Ships in 1853. More than a century into this period, in 1661, the Chinese rebel leader and Ming loyalist Koxinga ejected the Dutch from Formosa, now Taiwan, and even threatened Manila before he died suddenly the next year.

*

Jodocus Hondius's 'reduced' map of China (Amsterdam, 1607)

Asia's integration into global markets was, of course, not limited to the Manila galleon trade. In yet another manifestation of globalisation in this early period, Europeans – notably the Portuguese and then the Dutch – soon came to play a major role in Asia's regional and trans-

70

continental trade. European third-parties transported goods within Asia and also acted as intermediaries in the Chinese-Japanese silver trade.

While this commercial footprint was not itself an indication of either military or political power, it probably comes as no surprise that some on the ground harboured such delusions. In 1576, the governor of the Philippines, Francisco de Sande, wrote Philip II proposing an invasion of China, which he said 'would be very easy', requiring just a few thousand men:

> The equipments necessary for this expedition are four or
> six thousand men, armed with lances and arquebuses, and
> the ships, artillery, and necessary munitions. With two
> or three thousand men one can take whatever province
> he pleases, and through its ports and fleet render himself
> the most powerful on the sea. This will be very easy. In
> conquering one province, the conquest of all is made. The
> people would revolt immediately . . . In all the islands a
> great many corsairs live, from whom also we could obtain
> help for this expedition, as also from the Japanese, who are
> the mortal enemies of the Chinese. All would gladly take
> part in it.[6]

Philip was having none of it. There is a note in the margin of the report: 'Reply as to the receipt of this; and that, in what relates to the conquest of China, it is not fitting at the present time to discuss that matter. On the contrary, he must strive for the maintenance of friendship with the Chinese, and must not make any alliance with the pirates hostile to the Chinese, nor give that nation any just cause for indignation against us.'[7] Sande tried again in another letter in 1579, as did his successor, Diego de Ronquillo, a few years later. But the suggestions seem to have fallen on entirely deaf ears. And once the Manila galleon got going, these proposals seem never to have come up again.

Globalisation was considerably more balanced – economically and politically – between East and West in this first chapter than it was to be in the story's second. That is not to say, Philip II's stated intentions notwithstanding, that relations were very friendly, or that there was not any protracted shoving. The opportunities for trade and access to raw materials did indeed occasion military action and territorial expansion, but it was the Philippines and the rest of Southeast Asia, rather than the much more powerful China and Japan, that bore the brunt of this.

China was larger in territory, economy and population at the end of this period than at the beginning. The twenty-first century is not the West's first encounter with a rising China. Nor is this the first time the West has tried unsuccessfully to fit the entire world into a single overarching conceptual framework. Just as the advance of Western-led globalisation provides the validation for democracy and individual freedom, these values also become the philosophical justification for globalisation.

Sixteenth and seventeenth century globalisation was a consequence rather than an explicit objective of Spanish policy and commerce. But Spanish policy nevertheless had a conceptual framework of its own: Catholicism. To the modern eye, attempts at religious conversion can seem tangential and even detrimental to geopolitical advance and commercial gain. But without questioning the sincere beliefs of the adherents, there was a good deal of *realpolitik* in advancing Catholicism. Actions, however one-sided, could be presented as being in the interests of the other party. There was a feeling that shared values and beliefs made it easier to do business.

Converts also undermined existing hierarchies, loyalties and structures in both occupied territories and other countries. The resulting activities were often considered less than innocent by the governments of China and Japan. Complaints about 'interference in internal affairs' are not a uniquely modern phenomenon. The linking of ideology and policy could be a two-edged sword: just as democrats today question *realpolitik* alliances, Spanish clerics were among the most vociferous opponents of forced labour in colonial mines and agricultural estates.

Manila galleon-era Spain had a historical narrative

of its own: it had been progressively expanding and unifying for centuries – first the reconquista of the Iberian peninsula and then the conquest of an entire new world. Catholicism went hand-in-glove with this territorial and – once the wealth of the Americas came on stream – financial expansion, a success which both validated Catholicism and was in turn justified by it.

Ultimately, the Spanish narrative, not unlike the current Anglo-American narrative, ran up against the reality that is China. The Sino-Spanish story, and the Silver Way, went into abeyance for about 200 years. It is only in the last decade that the stirrings of a possible rebirth can be witnessed.

VII

Ruta Redux

'Men's fortunes are on a wheel, which in its turning
suffers not the same man to prosper for ever.'
– Herodotus

China is ever wont to surprise, but few recent developments seem to have caught observers as much off guard as the country's current foray into Latin America, including a dramatic proposal for a transcontinental railway traversing both the Amazon and the Andes. But rather than being entirely new, these admittedly still embryonic relationships are reflected in the Sino-Latin American trade of the sixteenth to eighteenth centuries.

Latin America, like much of the world, is currently experiencing a 'pivot to Asia', or perhaps it's really a pivot back. One canal ready see the possible beginnings of a modern Silver Way taking shape. There is, as history echoes down the centuries, considerable emphasis on transportation infrastructure and natural resources. China has been active for several years in mining and agricultural projects from Peru to Brazil. A high-speed rail project in Mexico was derailed due to problems in the tendering process. The Twin Ocean Railroad Connection is a 5000-kilometre high-speed rail project to connect the Atlantic coast of Brazil to the Pacific coast of Peru, through the Amazon and over the Andes. A controversial 50 billion US dollar project has also been tabled to dig a new canal connecting the Pacific and Atlantic via Nicaragua.

The engineering projects, in particular, are extremely ambitious from the engineering perspective and somewhat dubious from the financial point of view. Few of these projects have escaped criticism on environmental, political or social grounds. Nevertheless, as statements of intent, they speak very loudly.

*

The parallels between the Silver Way and the earlier Silk Road will surely not have escaped notice. The latter, which flourished for roughly two millennia, entered its final decline with the end of *pax mongolica* and the conquest of Constantinople by the Ottoman Turks. The Silver Way can in some ways be seen as the successor to the Silk Road. It was the disruption of the Silk Road in the fourteenth and then fifteenth centuries that catalysed the maritime space race discussed in Chapter I, and which led directly to the establishment of the Manila galleon trade.

In both cases, a single commodity acted to bind disparate regions and peoples; the trade routes thus created were both engines of development and conduits for culture, philosophies and religions. Much of Central Asian prosperity owed its existence to the Silk Road trade. In the latter period, the same could be said of Manila and the Philippines. Both New Spain and the Viceroyalty of Peru owed much of their importance to the mines that produced the silver that was in so much demand.

Spanish America became a developed and sophisticated place, with cities, universities, printing presses, writers, artists and other elements of high civilisation – all a century or two before Harvard or New York gained much traction. Spanish America was a product of the High Renaissance; the Renaissance was well over before English North America started to get going.

It was not only silk that travelled along the Silk Road: religions (Buddhism, Manichaeism, Christianity), and technology (e.g. paper-making) did, too. As we have seen, culture and religion similarly travelled over the Silver Way.

It was not just nostalgia that led Chinese President Xi Jinping to evoke a new Silk Road in the recent 'One Belt, One Road' initiatives, for the term conjures up a period well before the West and US-based multinational institutions began to dominate. Xi made a direct appeal to history in his announcement.[1]

The Silk Road provides an attractive paradigm for the arrangement of China's relations with its neighbours. It evokes a time when China was economically dominant but not hegemonic: Chinese interests were well-defined, but allowed other parties to prosper, as some – notably the Sogdians from what is now Central Asia – did mightily. The Silk Road was a time of shifting, overlapping alliances and hierarchical relationships, when a well-placed gift or granting of a privilege could allow China to keep its place at the centre of the political firmament. There is no need, the paradigm continues, for Western-dominated institutions such as the WTO, the World Bank and the IMF: China and the region will have their own.

The Silk Road – ironically a Western coinage dating from 1877 – has had good propagandists and has been fixed in popular and political imagination. The Pacific route also has historical validity and the potential to offer China a non-Anglo-American, if not quite non-Western, paradigm for arranging its relations with the countries to its east. The Silk Road went west from China over land. The Silver Way went east by sea. They are nevertheless fundamentally similar.

These global maritime trade routes predated British and then American global dominance. As a paradigm, the

Silver Way hearkens back to a time when the world's most important trade link was that between Spanish America and China, and when the West was led – politically and culturally – not by English-speaking countries but by those speaking what are now known as the Romance languages. The thirty-three members of the recently-formed China and the Community of Latin American and Caribbean States (CELAC) pointedly do not include the United States and Canada.

Conclusion

If Urdaneta is to globalisation what Columbus is to America, why has he come to be largely forgotten in the English-speaking world? Indeed, the Manila galleon, the silver trade and the role of the Spanish silver peso seem to be largely absent from Anglo-American history texts, except those specialising in the precise period or subject. This particular amnesia can be dated. The 'Indies' trade in general, and silver in particular, remain central to many of the arguments about economics in Adam Smith's *The Wealth of Nations*, published in 1776. But as the Spanish Empire receded from the scene, and English-speakers found they had other geopolitical and economic priorities, not least the industrial revolution, forgetfulness began to set in.

From the heights of American global dominance, the fork of history that led to the Spanish Empire seemed something of a cul-de-sac, tangentially relevant to further global progress. Two hundred and fifty years of Sino-Spanish trade was relegated – again, in the English-speaking world – to specialist journals whence they have only recently started to re-emerge.

*

'From that point, my eyes opened and I began to
understand that China was not as inaccessible as the
Portuguese had led us to believe . . . and that the bad
reputation of the Mandarins was more an invention of
the Portuguese than based on any reality . . . and that
when people went there, they were merely asked where
they came from and what they wanted and once this
was known, they left to come and go in peace . . .'
— Fr. Domingo de Salazar, Bishop of the Philippines,
in a letter to Philip II, 24 June 1590[1]

Urdaneta, who was a navigator, understood the importance of maps and charts. They told you where you were, where you had been, where you were going and how to get back. Unless, of course, like Columbus's charts, they didn't. The reality that Columbus found didn't agree with his charts, yet he spent the rest of his life trying to get reality to fit the chart rather than changing the chart to fit reality.

Twenty-first century China is to the prevailing Anglo-American historical narrative what the Americas were to Columbus's charts. A rising China – one of the world's largest economic powers, with a military able to project force and a political culture that predates the Enlightenment – does not fit the model. It is a world power increasingly willing to go its own way outside the structure of multinational institutions so painstakingly built up since the end of the Second World War. It is no surprise that China can seem bewildering.

China bewildered the Spanish of 450 years ago as well. But they would have at least recognised a China that restricted navigation, wanted and often succeeded in setting the terms of trade and did things in its own way and that was rarely amenable to either persuasion or the use of force – a China, in other words, that expected the rest of the world to accept it on its own terms.

Two and a half centuries of increasing Anglo-American dominance, a trend that only increased in the post-Second World War period, has not just meant political, military and economic pre-eminence; it has also meant the steady encroachment of laws, language, currency, interest rates, philosophy, business practices and general priorities into local prerogatives. What might this narrative predict for a twenty-first century containing a China which has returned to its *status quo ante*?

Even the most optimistic observers now realise that

today's resurgent China does not seem content to play the part that this narrative has scripted for it, nor to play a part in any script but one largely of its own writing. The alternatives are not happy ones. Terms emanating from both the Second World War and the Cold War have recently been bandied about in reference to possible future scenarios.

The Silver Way, however, offers a third possibility: globalisation with neither convergence nor major armed conflict, where the two sides integrate but remain apart. This third possibility is not one where one side progresses while the other is held back: rather, the parties are in equilibrium, albeit an unstable one, subject to disruption, changes in relative terms of trade, differing interests and objectives and more than occasional misunderstandings.

It is important to bring early-modern Asia back into the prevailing historical narrative, to update our maps by making them older. Once we do, many of the trends we now consider inevitable seem not to be trends at all. The link between the narrative of the Silver Way and the later Anglo-American narrative is silver, or rather the monetisation and integration of the world's economies via currency and financial markets. The link remains today in the form of the US dollar and the Chinese yuan, both of which are descended from the Spanish peso. If the Sino-American relationship really is the world's most important of the twenty-first century, then Americans need a conceptual structure that doesn't measure China's rise against an ill-fitting historical yardstick.

The coming mid-century need not look like the turn of the last century, nor, God forfend, like the mid-1900s. It might instead resemble the world's first globalisation at the turn of the seventeenth century: an East and West that have neither converged nor descended into uncomprehending enmity, but rather in precarious balance, simultaneously cooperating and seeking advantage.

Stories are best started at the beginning. This one – the story of our increasingly integrated world – begins in the Pacific around 1565 and not, as conventional wisdom often has it, in the Western Europe of the mid-eighteenth century.

TIMELINE

1492	**Christopher Columbus lands in the New World**
1513	Vasco Núñez de Balboa crosses the isthmus of Panama to set sight on the Pacific
1521	Hernán Cortés conquers Mexico-Tenochtitlán
1519–1522	Magellan-Elcano circumnavigation; Magellan is killed in the Philippines
1522	Gómez Espinosa, of the same expedition, makes first failed attempt to return eastwards
1525–1526	García Jofre de Loaísa expedition to the Spice Islands; Urdaneta is shipwrecked
1527–1529	Álvaro de Saavedra is also unable to return eastwards after two attempts.
1535	**Establishment of the Viceroyalty of New Spain (Nueva España) in Mexico**
1537–1538	Hernando de Grijalva expedition across the Pacific; crew mutinies

1542–1545	Ruy López de Villalobos expedition; the Philippines named
1543	Bernardo de la Torre makes fourth failed attempt to return eastwards
1545	Iñigo Ortiz de Retes makes fifth failed attempt to return eastwards; New Guinea is named
1545	**Discovery of silver at Potosí**
1551	Founding of the first university in Mexico (Royal and Pontifical University)
1564–1565	**Miguel López de Legazpi / Andrés de Urdaneta expedition to the Philippines**
1565	**Urdaneta discovers the *tornaviaje***
1571	Legazpi founds Manila
1573	The first cargo of Chinese products sails to Mexico
1730s	**First milled Spanish dollars produced**
1776	Adam Smith publishes *The Wealth of Nations*
1815	**Last Manila galleon (the 'Magallanes') sails from Acapulco**

NOTES

Prologue

1   Blair & Robertson, vol. 2, available online at http://www.gutenberg.
    org/ebooks/13280.

I

1   George Orwell, *As I Please*, 4 February 1944, found at: http://or-
    well.ru/library/articles/As_I_Please/english/eaip_01.
2   Authors' translation of 'Documentos relativos al descubrimiento
    de las islas del Poniente; Archivo General de Indias, PATRO-
    NATO, 23, R.12' in the *Archivos Españoles* and can be found
    here: http://pares.mcu.es/ParesBusquedas/servlets/Control_
    servlet?accion=4&txt_accion_origen=2&txt_id_desc_ud=121750.
3   Authors' translation; original may be found at: https://archive.org/
    stream/coleciondocument02seririch/coleciondocument02seri-
    rich_djvu.txt.
4   Blair & Robertson, vol. 2
5   Blair & Robertson, vol. 3, available at http://www.gutenberg.org/
    ebooks/13616.
6   Ibid.

II

1   Authors' translation; original may be found at: https://www.upf.
    edu/asia/projectes/che/s16/felipe.htm.
2   Manel Ollé, *La invención de China: Percepciones y estrategias
    filipinas respecto a China durante el siglo XVI*, Harrassowitz Verlag,
    Wiesbaden, 2000.

3   Blair & Robertson, vol. 3.

4   Benito Legarda, Jr., 'Two and a Half Centuries of the Galleon
    Trade', Philippine Studies vol. 3, no. 4, 1955.

5   *Sucesos de las Islas Filipinas*, Antonio de Morga; Mexico, 1609
    from Blair & Robertson, vol. 16. Sucesos was also issued by Blair
    & Robertson separately, The Arthur H Clark Company, 1907, and
    is available on Gutenberg.org.

6   The term used for Chinese, especially merchants; it might derive
    from the Hokkien *seng-li* (生理).

7   Blair & Robertson, vol. 7. Available at http://www.gutenberg.org/
    ebooks/13701.

8   Blair & Robertson, vol. 29. Available at http://www.gutenberg.org/
    ebooks/38748.

9   This material is covered in several sources, but a particularly
    complete account is in 'The History of the Manila Galleon Trade'
    by Catherine Lugar, in *Archaeological Report of The Recovery of
    The Manila Galleon Nuestra Señora de la Concepción, Pacific Sea
    Resources*, 1990, p. 31.

10 Benito Legarda, Jr., op. cit.

11 Efren B. Isorean, 'Maritime Disasters in Spanish Philippines: The
    Manila-Acapulco Galleons, 1565-1815', *International Journal of
    Asia Pacific Studies: IJAPS*, vol. 11, no. 1, 53–83, 2015.

12 Giovanni Francesco Gemelli Careri (see Bibliography). These
    passages are from the Churchill 1732, edition vol. 4 pp. 468.

13 Ibid, pp. 468.

III

1   Authors' translation. Original can be found here http://shemer.
    mslib.huji.ac.il/lib/W/ebooks/001531300.pdf.

2   Careri, op. Cit. p.479.

3   Careri, op. Cit. p.480.

4   Alexander von Humboldt, *Political Essay on the Kingdom of
    New Spain*, 1811.

5   *Informatory memorial addressed to the king*. Juan Grau y Monfal-
    cón; Madrid, 1637, in Blair & Robertson, vol. 27.

6   Lugar, pp. 18, 20.

7   Cinta Krahe, *Chinese Porcelain in Habsburg Spain*, Centro de
    Estudios Europa Hispánica, 2016, pp 276–77 and Natale Zappia,
    'Porcelain and Cocoa: The Pacific Rim and the Early Modern World
    Economy' in 'Commodities in World History, 1450-1950': a Project
    of the UCSC Center for World History, http://cwh.ucsc.edu/com-
    modities.html.

8   Shirley Ganse, *Chinese Porcelain: An Export to the World*, Joint
     Publishing, 2008, pp. 80–1.
9   Blair & Robertson, vol. 27. Available at http://www.gutenberg.org/
     ebooks/26004.
10   Ibid.
11   Ibid.
12   Alexander von Humboldt, op. cit.
13   This is related in several places, including Homer H. Dubs and
     Robert S. Smith, 'Chinese in Mexico City in 1635', *The Far
     Eastern Quarterly*, vol. 1, no. 4 (August 1942), pp. 387–9.
14   Thomas Gage, The English-American: A New Survey of the
     West Indies, 1648, pp. 84–5 in the RoutledgeCurzon edition
     (see Bibliography for details).
15   Blair & Robertson, vol. 2.

IV

1   Blair & Robertson, vol. 2.
2   *The Encomienda in New Spain: The Beginning of Spanish Mexico*
     by Lesley Byrd Simpson, p 226–7; an 1881 edition can be found
     here https://archive.org/details/donfrayjuandezu00icazgoog.
3   Bernardo de Balbuena, *La Grandeza Mexicana* [The Grandeur
     of Mexico City], 1604. A transcription may be found online
     http://www.ellibrototal.com/ltotal/ficha.jsp?idLibro=2732.
4   Gage, op. cit. p.84.
5   Ibid, p. 85.
6   The Spanish translates loosely to 'History of the most notable
     things, rites and customs of the great kingdom of China'.
7   By comparison, this was three-quarters of a century after the first
     books were printed in Mexico, yet still three decades before the
     first book was published in what is now the United States (*The
     Whole Booke of Psalmes Faithfully, Translated into English Metre*,
     published in Cambridge, Massachusetts in 1640).
8   "Sátira filosófica" by Sor Juana Inés de la Cruz, published in *Inun-
     dación castálida* (Madrid, 1689). Authors' translation.
9   Slack, 'Sinifying New Spain', p. 8–9, 12–13.
10   Bernardo de Balbuena, op. cit.
11   Ibid.
12   Careri, op. cit. p.405.
13   The Spanish translates loosely to 'Rich mirror of the clear heart'.
14   Matthew Y. Chen, 'Unsung Trailblazers of China-West Cultural
     Encounter', found at: http://personal.vu.nl/p.j.peverelli/Chen.html.

V

1   Adam Smith, *An Inquiry Into the Nature and Causes of the Wealth of Nations*. Available from Gutenberg.org.

2   Blair & Robertson, vol. 3.

3   Ibid.

4   Dennis O. Flynn & Arturo Giráldez, 'Born with a "Silver Spoon": The Origin of World Trade in 1571', *Journal of World History*, vol. 6, no. 2, 1995, University of Hawai'i Press.

5   Ibid.

6   The coat of arms can be found online: https://commons.wiki-media.org/wiki/File:Escudo_otorgado_por_Carlos_V,_dada_en_Ulma_el_28_de_enero_de_1547.JPG.

7   Blair & Robertson, vol. 22. Available at http://www.gutenberg.org/ebooks/16297.

8   'Silver Spoon', op. cit.

9   The coat of arms can be found online: http://www.eldiario.net/noticias/2015/2015_11/nt151110/nuevoshorizontes.php?n=10&-los-blasones-de-potosi-de-antanio.

10 Hugh Thomas, *World Without End: The Global Empire of Philip II*, Penguin, 2014.

11 Ken Pomeranz & Bin Wong, 'The Silver Trade, Part 1', found at: http://afe.easia.columbia.edu/chinawh/web/s5/s5_4.html.

12 Charles Ralph Boxer, *The Christian Century in Japan: 1549-1650*, University of California Press, 1951, p. 426; also in 'Plata es Sangre'.

13 Ibid.

14 'Silver Spoon', p. 207.

15 *Wealth of Nations*, op. cit.

16 Timothy Brook, 'Vermeer's Hat: The Seventeenth Century and the Dawn of the Global World', Bloomsbury, 2008, pp. 176–7.

17 Flynn & Giraldez, 'Cycles of Silver, Globalization as historical process', *World Economics*, vol. 3, no. 2, April–June, 2002.

18 *Metals, Monies, and Markets in Early Modern Societies: East Asian and Global Perspectives Monies, Markets, and Finance in China and East Asia*, vol. 1, Thomas Hirzel, Nanny Kim (eds.), LIT Verlag Münster, 2008.

VI

1   'Cycles of Silver', op. cit.

2   Ibid.

3   Manel Ollé, 'Interacción y conflicto en el parián de Manila', *Illes i Imperis*, 2008: Num. 10/11.

4   *Wealth of Nations*, op. cit.

5   Geoffrey Parker, 'The Military Revolution: Military Innovation and

the Rise of the West, 1500-1800', Cambridge University Press, 1966, p. 132.

6   Blair & Robertson, vol. 4.
7   Ibid.

VII
1   'History, over the past millennia,' said Xi, 'has witnessed ancient civilisations appear and thrive along the Yellow and Yangtze Rivers, the Indus, the Ganges, the Euphrates and the Tigris River, as well as in Southeast Asia, each adding its own splendour to the progress of human civilisation. Today, Asia has proudly maintained its distinct diversity and still nurtures all the civilisations, ethnic groups and religions in this big Asian family.' From the 'Towards a Community of Common Destiny and A New Future for Asia' keynote speech by Xi Jinping at the Boao Forum for Asia Annual Conference 2015.

Conclusion
1   Blair & Robertson, vol. 7.

BIBLIOGRAPHY

The list of books that follows is not meant to be complete, but includes primary sources used by the authors as references. While many works are recompiled in different editions, original resources are listed.

Balbuena, Bernardo, *La Grandeza Mexicana (The Grandeur of Mexico City)*, 1604, http://www.ellibrototal. com/ltotal/ficha.jsp?idLibro=2732.

Boxer, Charles Ralph, 'Plata Es Sangre: Sidelights on the Drain of Spanish-American Silver in the Far East, 1550–1700', *Philippine Studies*, vol. 18, no. 3, 1970.

—, *The Christian Century in Japan: 1549-1650*, University of California Press, 1951.

Brook, Timothy, 'Vermeer's Hat: The Seventeenth Century and the Dawn of the Global World', Bloomsbury, 2008.

Careri, Giovanni Francesco Gemelli, *Giro del Mondo,*

A Collection of Voyages and Travels: Some Now First Printed from Original Manuscripts by Awnsham Churchill and John Churchill, vol. 4, 1732.

Flynn and Giráldez, Dennis O., Arturo, 'Born with a "Silver Spoon": The Origin of World Trade in 1571', *Journal of World History*, vol. 6, no. 2, University of Hawai'i Press, 1995.

Gage, Thomas, *The English-American: A New Survey of the West Indies, 1648.*

Legarda. Jr., Benito, 'Two and a Half Centuries of the Galleon Trade', *Philippine Studies*, vol. 3, no. 4, 1955.

Lugar, Catherine, 'The History of the Manila Galleon Trade', *Archaeological Report of The Recovery of The Manila Galleon Nuestra Señora de la Concepción*, Pacific Sea Resources, 1990.

Secondary Sources and Further Reading

Secondary sources can be divided into four broad categories: those that cover the Manila galleon; survey works on the period that discuss globalisation; those that deal with specialised matters such as migration and culture; and those that cover silver. Of course, because the issue cuts across so many themes and countries, a great many works intersect with the issues here.

Manila Galleon and Trade

La empresa de China: de la Armada Invencible al Galeón de Manila, Manel Ollé, El Acantilado, Barcelona, 2002.

La ruta española a China, Carlos Martínez Shaw & Marina Alfonso Mola (eds.), El Viso, Madrid, 2007.

Les Philippines et le Pacifique des Ibériques (XVIe, XVIIe, XVIIIe siècles), Pierre Chaunu, SEVPEN, 2 vols., 1960 & 1966.

'Mexico, Peru, and the Manila Galleon', William Lytle Schurz, *The Hispanic American Historical Review*, vol. 1, no. 4, November 1918.

'Silk and Silver: Macau, Manila and Trade in the China Seas in the Sixteenth Century', John Villiers, *Journal of the Hong Kong Branch of the Royal Asiatic Society*, vol. 20, 1980.

The Manila Galleon, William Lytle Schurz, Historical Conservation Society, 1939; E.P. Dutton & Co., 1959.

The Spanish Lake, O.H.K. Spate, Australia National University Press, 1979.

Globalisation

ReOrient: Global Economy in the Asian Age, Andre Gunder Frank, University of California Press, 1998.

The Age of Trade: The Manila Galleons and the Dawn of the Global Economy, Arturo Giráldez, Rowman & Littlefield, 2015.

The Eagle and the Dragon: Globalization and European Dreams of Conquest in China and America in the Sixteenth Century, Serge Gruzinski, Polity Press, 2014.

The Great Divergence: China, Europe, and the Making of the Modern World Economy, Kenneth Pomeranz, Princeton University Press, 2000.

1493: Uncovering the New World Columbus Created, Charles C. Mann, Alfred A. Knopf, 2011.

Migration, Culture, General History, etc.

'Asia llega a América. Migración e influencia cultural asiática en Nueva España (1565–1815)', Rubén Carrillo, *Asiadémica*: no. 3, January 2014.

Descubrimientos españoles en el Mar del Sur, Amancio Landín Carrasco et al., 3 vols., Editorial Naval, Madrid, 1992.

'Orientalizing New Spain: Perspectives of Asian Influence in Colonial Mexico', Edward R. Slack, delivered at Transpacific & Transoceanic Exchanges, Brown University, December 2010, https://www.brown.edu/conference/asia-pacific/sites/brown.edu.Conference.Asia-Pacific/files/apma-Slack.doc.

'Sinifying New Spain: Cathay's Influence on Colonial

Mexico via the *Nao* de China' by Edward R. Slack, Jr.,
in *The Chinese in Latin America and the Caribbean*,
ed. Walton Look Lai, Chee Beng Tan, Brill, 2010.

*The Great Ship From Amacon: Annals of Macao and the
Old Japan Trade, 1555–1640*, Charles Ralph Boxer,
Centro de Estudios Históricos Ultramarinos, 1959.

Silver

'Born with a "Silver Spoon": The Origin of World Trade
in 1571', Dennis O. Flynn & Arturo Giráldez, *Journal
of World History*, vol. 6, no. 2, 1995, University of
Hawai'i Press.

'Cycles of Silver, Globalization as historical process',
Dennis O. Flynn & Arturo Giráldez, *World Economics*, vol. 3, no. 2, April–June 2002.

*Fountain of Fortune: Money and Monetary Policy in
China, 1000–1700*, Richard von Glahn, University of
California Press, 1996.

'Silk for Silver: Manila–Macao Trade in the 17th Century', Dennis O. Flynn & Arturo Giráldez, *Philippine
Studies*, vol. 44, no. 1, 1996.

'The inflow of American silver into China from the late
Ming to the mid-Ch'ing Period', Chuan Hang-sheng,
*Journal of the Institute of Chinese Studies of the Chi-
nese University of Hong Kong*, vol. 2, 1969.

ILLUSTRATIONS

All illustrations are of items in Juan José Morales's personal collection except where indicated below:

P12 España Ministerio de Educación, Cultura y Deporte. Archivo General de Indias. Patronato, 23, R.12

P13 España Ministerio de Educación, Cultura y Deporte. Archivo General de Indias. Patronato, 1, N.6, R.1

P22 John Carter Brown Library at Brown University

P33 Tom Christensen, from *1616: The World in Motion*, Counterpoint Press, 2012

P35 Trustees of the Boston Public Library

P53 Tom Christensen, from *1616: The World in Motion*, Counterpoint Press, 2012

P60, 61, 62 Heritage Auctions

ACKNOWLEDGEMENTS

The authors would (jointly) like to thank Germán Muñoz, erstwhile president of the Mexican Chamber of Commerce in Hong Kong for his support of all Ibero-American cultural and intellectual activities in Hong Kong, and for his enthusiasm for the Silver Way concept. They would also like to thank Kerry Brown, Manel Ollé, Salvatore Babones and Nicholas Gordon for taking the time to read the work while it was in manuscript form, and likewise Imogen Liu of Penguin China for her many valuable editorial comments and suggestions; James Pach of *The Diplomat*, who published one of the first articles on this subject on the 450th anniversary of the *tornaviaje*; and the Boston Public Library, John Carter Brown Library at Brown University, Tom Christensen and Heritage Auctions for their gracious permission to use illustrations.

Juan José Morales would like to extend his personal

thanks to Jonathan Wattis of Wattis Fine Arts and the Philippine Map Collectors Society, and César Guillén-Nuñez of the Matteo Ricci Institute of Macao, who introduced him to this subject twenty years ago. He would also like to thank Noemí Espinosa Fernández of the Hispanic Society of America in New York and León Gómez Rivas of Universidad Europea de Madrid, both of whom assisted with the bibliography.

PENGUIN
SPECIALS

A Billion Voices

DAVID MOSER

China's Search for a Common Language

Mandarin, Guoyu or Putonghua? 'Chinese' is a language known by many names, and China is a country home to many languages. Since the turn of the twentieth century linguists and politicians have been on a mission to create a common language for China. From the radical intellectuals of the May Fourth Movement, to leaders such as Chiang Kai-shek and Mao Zedong, all fought linguistic wars to push the boundaries of language reform. Now, Internet users take the Chinese language in new and unpredictable directions. David Moser tells the remarkable story of China's language unification agenda and its controversial relationship with modern politics, challenging our conceptions of what it means to speak and be Chinese.

David Moser is a scholar of linguistics and currently serves as Academic Director of CET Chinese Studies at Beijing Capital Normal University. He has taught courses in Translation Theory and Psycholinguistics, and is an active commentator on Chinese media in both Chinese and English.

'Could it be true that "Chinese" is many languages, in fact? That they differ from one another as much as English, French, and German do? That "Mandarin" is a fairly recent invention? That Chinese people have disagreed, sometimes heatedly, about what the features and uses of Mandarin should be? This witty little book shows that all of this is so. A banquet of history and ethnography is salted with nuance that the author has drawn from several years' work with Central Chinese Television.'
Perry Link, author of An Anatomy of Chinese: Rhythm, Metaphor, Politics

'If you want to know what the language situation of China is on the ground and in the trenches, and you only have time to read one book, this is it. A veritable tour de force, in just a little over a hundred pages, David Moser has filled this brilliant volume with linguistic, political, historical, and cultural data that are both reliable and enlightening. Written with captivating wit and exacting expertise, A Billion Voices is a masterpiece of clear thinking and incisive exposition.'
Victor H. Mair, American sinologist, professor of Chinese language and literature at the University of Pennsylvania and author of The Columbia History of Chinese Literature

PENGUIN
SPECIALS

The People's Bard

NANCY PELLEGRINI

How China Made Shakespeare its Own

The story of Shakespeare in China is one of cultural blending and reinvention. Peopled by devoted evangelists, theatre directors and dogged interpreters intent on bridging divisions of language and politics, it tracks the trajectory of modern Chinese history and the development of theatre arts. Four hundred years after Shakespeare's death, Nancy Pellegrini pulls back the curtain on how the Bard of Avon rose from inauspicious Chinese beginnings to become the People's Bard, exploring traditional opera-style Shakespeare productions, decades of Marxist interpretations, revolutionary translation methods and more.

Nancy Pellegrini is a Beijing-based author, journalist and photographer. Since 2006, she has worked as the Fine Arts editor for *Time Out Beijing*, specialising in Asian theater and music. Her articles have appeared in *South China Morning Post and Gramophone UK*.